SIMONE BILES

BY LEIGH LEWIS

AMICUS LEARNING

Inspire is published by
Amicus Learning, an imprint of Amicus
P.O. Box 227
Mankato, MN 56002
www.amicuspublishing.us

Editor: Ana Brauer
Series Designer: Kathleen Petelinsek
Book Designer and Photo Researcher: Emily Dietz

Library of Congress Cataloging-in-Publication Data
Names: Lewis, Leigh, author.
Title: Simone Biles / Leigh Lewis.
Description: Mankato, MN : Amicus Learning, 2026. | Series: Inspire | Includes bibliographical references and index. | Audience: Ages 5–9 | Audience: Grades 2–3 | Summary: "Learn about gymnastics star Simone Biles and her accomplishments in an engaging profile packed with photos and fact-filled text suitable for young readers. Includes table of contents, glossary, further resources, and index"— Provided by publisher.
Identifiers: LCCN 2024044036 (print) | LCCN 2024044037 (ebook) | ISBN 9798892005227 (library binding) | ISBN 9798892005760 (paperback) | ISBN 9798892006309 (ebook)
Subjects: LCSH: Biles, Simone 1997—Juvenile literature. | Women gymnasts—United States—Biography—Juvenile literature. | African American women athletes—United States—Biography—Juvenile literature. | African American women Olympic athletes—United States—Biography—Juvenile literature. | Women Olympic athletes—Mental health—Juvenile literature. | Presidential Medal of Freedom—Juvenile literature.
Classification: LCC GV460.2.B55 L495 2026 (print) | LCC GV460.2.B55 (ebook) | DDC 796.44092 [B]—dc23/eng/20241121
LC record available at https://lccn.loc.gov/2024044036
LC ebook record available at https://lccn.loc.gov/2024044037

Photo Credits: Associated Press/Bildbyran/Sipa USA, cover, Eliot Blondet/Abaca/Sipa USA, 16, Kamil Krzaczynski, 19, Kyodo, 4, Oliver Contreras/SIPA USA, 20, Yves Logghe, 8; Getty Images/Houston Chronicle/Hearst Newspapers, 6–7, Maddie Meyer, 12–13, Marijan Murat/picture alliance, 5, Robert Gauthier, 18, Tim Clayton - Corbis, 11, 14–15

Printed in India

Table of Contents

Simone Biles is the best female gymnast in the world.

The G.O.A.T.

Simone Biles runs down the runway. She jumps off the vault. She flips backwards twice. She sticks the landing! The crowd cheers loudly. Biles is the greatest gymnast of all time.

AWARD WINNER

Biles has 30 World Championship Medals. This is more than any other gymnast.

Early Life

When Biles was six, her grandparents adopted her and her sister. She jumped, twisted, and flipped on their trampoline. One day, she went to a gym in Houston, Texas. She watched the gymnasts. She copied their moves.

gym in Houston, Texas until she was 17.

The Boulder
The Boulder
HANDSPRING TRAINER

Biles won her first championship medal when she was 16.

Junior Champion

Biles worked very hard. She was homeschooled. This gave her more time to practice. In 2011, she competed in her first Junior National event. She was 14. In 2013, she won her first World Championship medal.

DID YOU KNOW?
When Biles was young, she learned she had **ADHD**.

All-Around Star

There are four gymnastics events for women. These are the floor exercise, balance beam, uneven bars, and vault. Many gymnasts choose one event. They become **experts** at it. Not Biles. She competes in all four of them.

Biles often does difficult moves to earn more points.

Changing Course

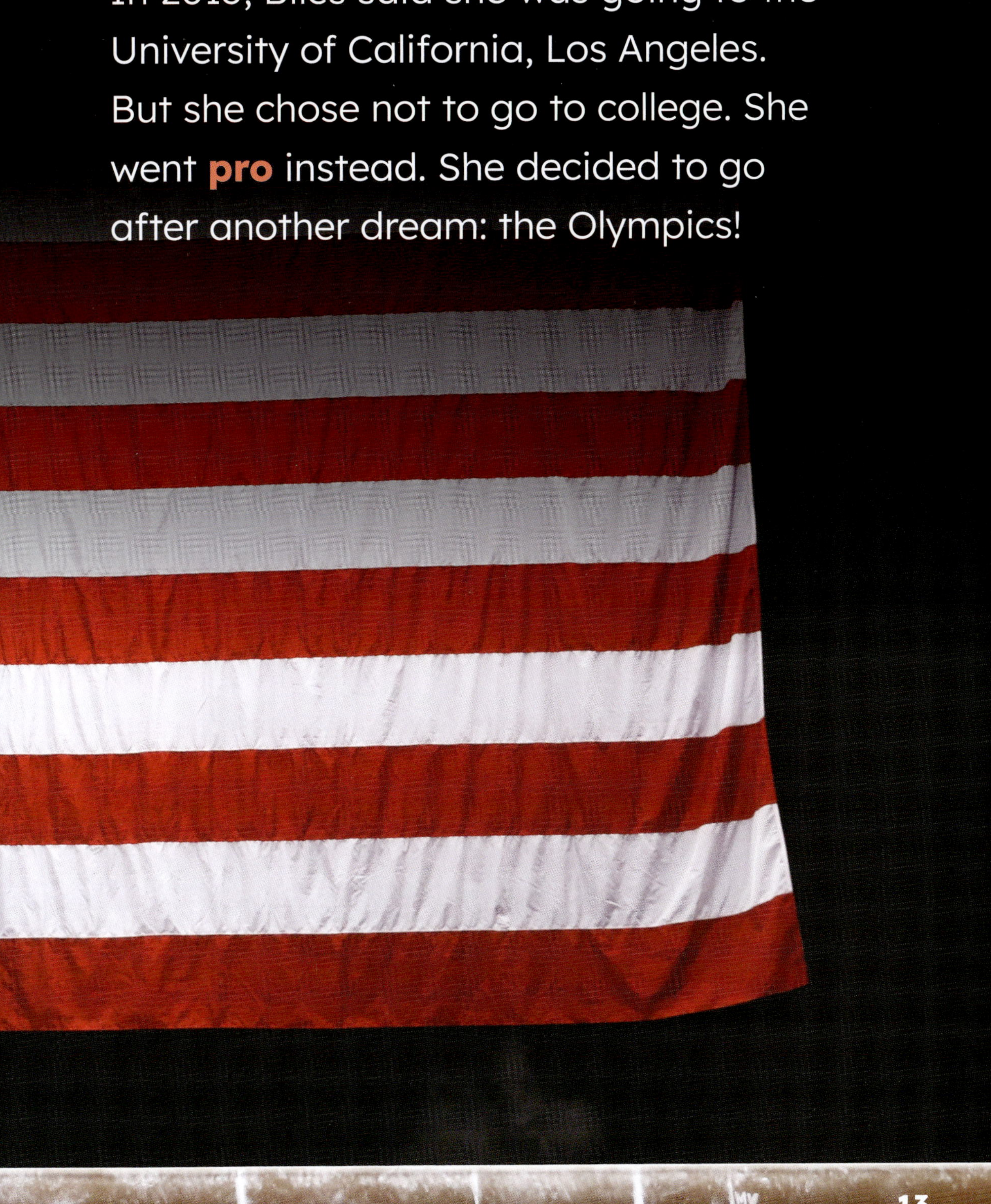

In 2015, Biles said she was going to the University of California, Los Angeles. But she chose not to go to college. She went **pro** instead. She decided to go after another dream: the Olympics!

Biles poses with one of her gold medals after the 2024 Paris Olympics.

Going for Gold

Biles is an Olympic superstar. She won five medals at the 2016 Rio Olympics. At the 2020 Tokyo games, she won a silver and a bronze medal. She later dropped out because of physical and mental health concerns. In 2024, she made a comeback. She won four medals!

Biles performs the
Biles II floor exercise
at the 2024 Olympics.

New Moves

Elements are moves done in gymnastics. Some are named after athletes. These athletes perform them for the first time at an international competition. Biles has five moves named after her. Two are floor exercises. Two are on the vault. One is on the balance beam.

DID YOU KNOW?
The moves named after Biles are called "the Biles" or "the Biles II."

Family

In 2023, Biles married football player Jonathan Owens. He plays for the Chicago Bears. They are both pro athletes who support each other. They have two French bulldogs named Lilo and Rambo.

A fan made cardboard cutouts of the couple's dogs.

Biles goes to football games to watch her husband play.

President Biden said Biles is the best of America.

Speaking Up

Biles speaks up for other athletes. She talks about mental health and **abuse**. In 2022, President Biden awarded Biles the Presidential Medal of Freedom. It is the highest **civilian** honor in the United States.

DID YOU KNOW?
Biles was the youngest living person ever to earn the Medal of Freedom. She was 25.

SUPER STATS

SIMONE ARIANNE BILES

Nicknames: $imoney

Birthday: March 14, 1997

Birthplace: Columbus, OH

Hometown: Spring, TX

ACCOMPLISHMENTS

Most decorated gymnast in history

11 Olympic Medals: 7 gold, 2 silver, 2 bronze

30 World Championship medals: 23 gold, 4 silver, 3 bronze

Five elements named for her: The Biles I and II (vault), The Biles I and II (floor), The Biles (beam)

ESPY Award for Best Comeback Athlete: 2024

Laureus World Sportswoman of the Year: 2017, 2019, 2020

GLOSSARY

abuse Cruel treatment of a person, either with words or physical actions.

ADHD Attention-Deficit/ Hyperactive Disorder. A brain disorder where someone has trouble staying focused and sitting still.

civilian A person who is not serving in the military or the police.

element A single move in gymnastics.

expert A person who has a lot of experience or a special skill in something.

pro Short for professional. An athlete paid to compete in sports.

READ MORE

Cox Cannons, Heather. **What You Never Knew About Simone Biles.** North Mankato, MN: Spark, 2023.

Sabelko, Rebecca. **Simone Biles.** Minneapolis, MN: Bellwether Media, 2023.

ON THE WEB

Olympics Simone Biles
https://olympics.com/en/athletes/simone-biles

Simone Biles Official Website
https://simonebiles.com

INDEX

About the Author

Leigh Lewis is a children's author who loves her three kids, traveling, pickleball, and telling stories. She has lived in the US, Russia, Japan, England, Greece, and Turkey. Check out her books at leighlewisbooks.com.